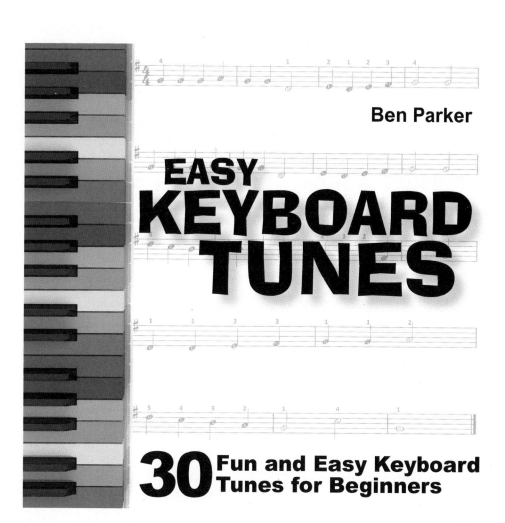

Ben Parker

EASY KEYBOARD TUNES

30 Fun and Easy Keyboard Tunes for Beginners

Author: Ben Parker
Editor: Alison McNicol
First published in 2014 by Kyle Craig Publishing
This version updated Dec 2014
Text and illustration copyright © 2014 Kyle Craig Publishing
Design: Julie Anson
Music set by Ben Parker using Sibelius software
ISBN: 978-1-908707-35-2
A CIP record for this book is available from the British Library.
A Kyle Craig Publication
www.kyle-craig.com
All Rights Reserved.

No part of this publication may be reproduced, stored in a retrieval system or transmitted by any form or by any means, electronic, recording or otherwise without the prior permission in writing from the publishers.

Unauthorised reproduction of any part of this publication by any means including photocopying is an infringement of copyright.

Contents

4   Humpty Dumpty

5   It's Raining / London Bridge

6   Drunken Sailor

7   Skip To My Lou / Scarborough Fair

8   My Old Man

9   Scotland The Brave

10   Home On The Range

11   Old MacDonald

12   Comin' Round The Mountain

13   Hush Little Baby / Clementine

14   All Things Bright And Beautiful

15   Song Of The Volga Boatmen / Dear Liza

16   Amazing Grace / My Bonnie

17   I Saw Three Ships / Au Clare De La Lune

18   Swing Low, Sweet Chariot

19   Kumbaya

20   Streets Of Laredo

21   Silent Night

22   Oh, Susanna

23   Ode To Joy / Drink To Me Only

24   We Wish You A Merry Christmas

25   Oh Little Town Of Bethlehem

26   Good King Wenceslas

27   We Three Kings Of Orient Are

Humpty Dumpty

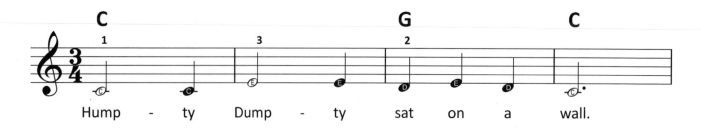

Hump - ty Dump - ty sat on a wall.

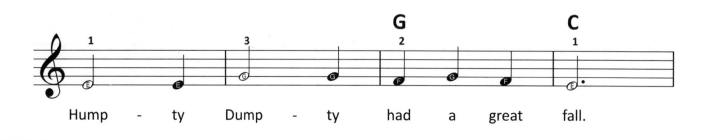

Hump - ty Dump - ty had a great fall.

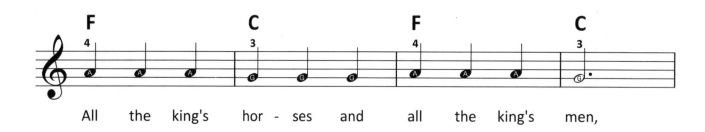

All the king's hor - ses and all the king's men,

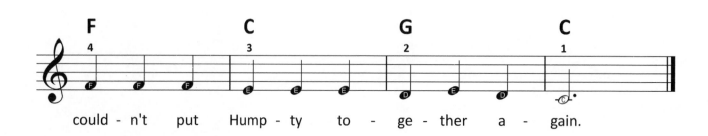

could - n't put Hump - ty to - ge - ther a - gain.

It's Raining

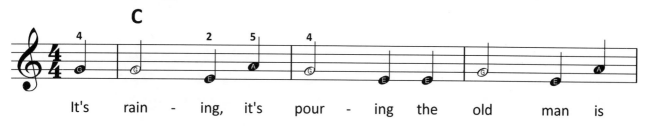

It's rain - ing, it's pour - ing the old man is

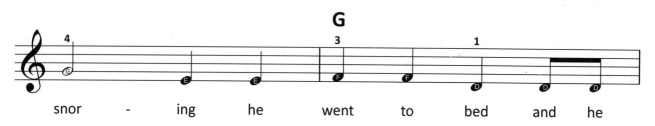

snor - ing he went to bed and he

bumped his head and he could-nt get up in the morn - ing. -

London Bridge

Lon - don Bridge is fall - ing down, fall - ing down, fall - ing down

Lon - don Bridge is fall - ing down, my fair la - dy.

Drunken Sailor

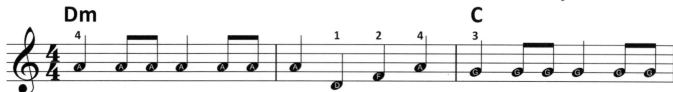

What shall we do with the drunk - en sail - or, what shall we do with the

drunk - en sail - or, what shall we do with the drunk - en sail - or

ear - ly in the morn - ing? Hoo - ray up she ri - ses,

hoo - ray up she ri - ses, hoo - ray

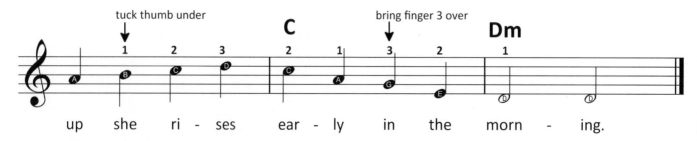

up she ri - ses ear - ly in the morn - ing.

Skip To My Lou

Skip, skip, skip to my Lou. Skip, skip, skip to my Lou.

Skip, skip, skip to my Lou. Skip to my Lou, my dar - ling.

Scarborough Fair

Are you going to Scar - bo rough fair? Par - sley,

sage, rose - ma - ry and thyme. Re - mem - ber me to

one who lives there._____ She once

was a true love of mine._____

7

My Old Man

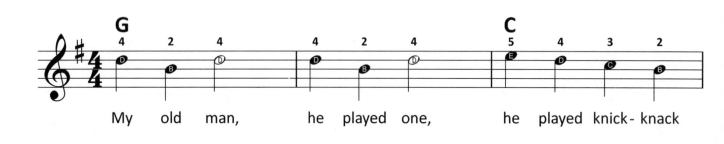

My old man, he played one, he played knick- knack

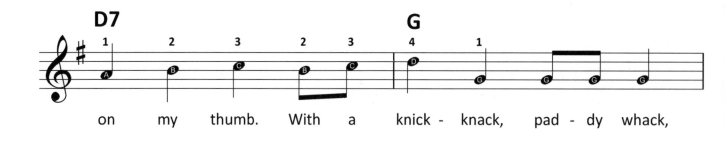

on my thumb. With a knick - knack, pad - dy whack,

give the dog a bone. This old man came roll - ing home.

Scotland The Brave

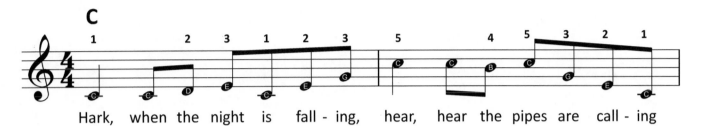

Hark, when the night is fall - ing, hear, hear the pipes are call - ing

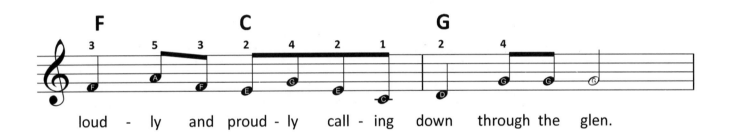

loud - ly and proud - ly call - ing down through the glen.

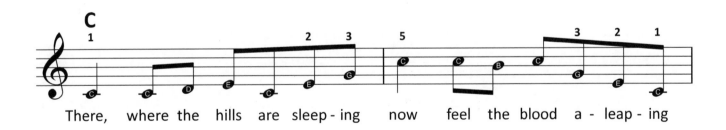

There, where the hills are sleep - ing now feel the blood a - leap - ing

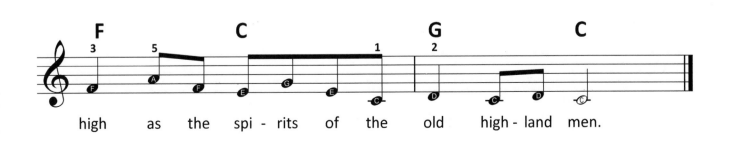

high as the spi - rits of the old high - land men.

Home On The Range

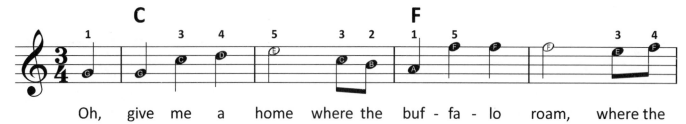

Oh, give me a home where the buf - fa - lo roam, where the

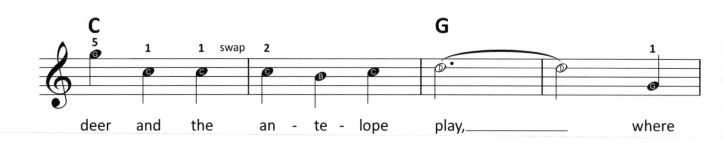

deer and the an - te - lope play,_____ where

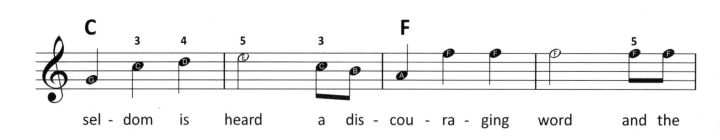

sel - dom is heard a dis - cou - ra - ging word and the

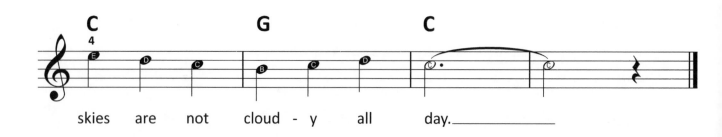

skies are not cloud - y all day._____

Old MacDonald

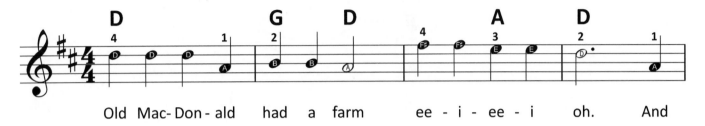

Old Mac-Don-ald had a farm ee - i - ee - i oh. And

on that farm he had some chi-ckens ee - i - ee - i

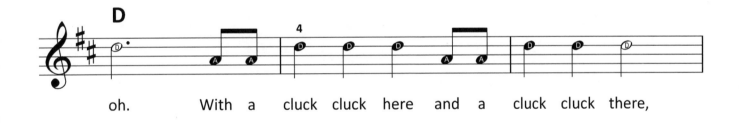

oh. With a cluck cluck here and a cluck cluck there,

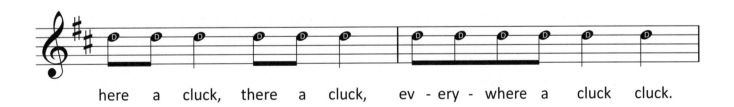

here a cluck, there a cluck, ev - ery - where a cluck cluck.

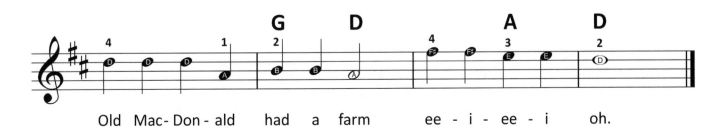

Old Mac-Don-ald had a farm ee - i - ee - i oh.

Comin' Round The Mountain

She'll be   com - in' round   the moun tain when she   comes.   She'll be

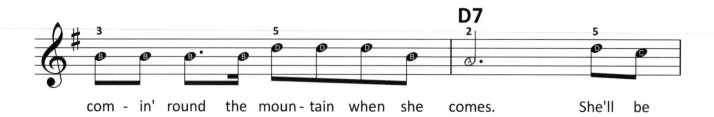

com - in' round   the moun - tain when   she   comes.   She'll be

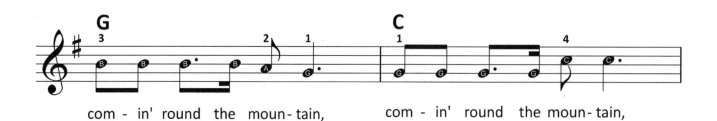

com - in' round   the moun - tain,   com - in' round   the moun - tain,

com - in' round   the moun - tain when she   comes.

Hush Little Baby

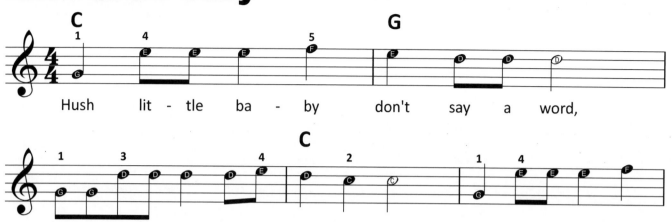

Hush lit - tle ba - by don't say a word,

ma-ma's gon- na buy you a mock - ing bird. And if that mock - ing

bird don't sing, ma-ma's gon- na buy you a dia - mond ring.

Clementine

Oh my dar - ling, oh my dar - ling, oh my

dar - ling Cle - men - tine; you are lost and gone for -

ev - er dread - ful sor - ry Cle - men - tine.

All Things Bright And Beautiful

All things bright and beau - ti - ful, all crea - tures great and

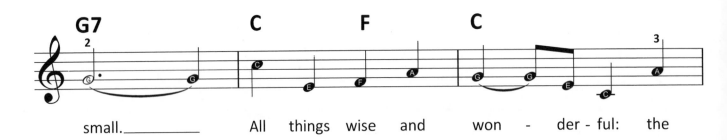

small._____ All things wise and won - der - ful: the

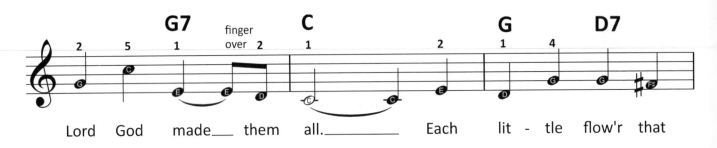

Lord God made___ them all._____ Each lit - tle flow'r that

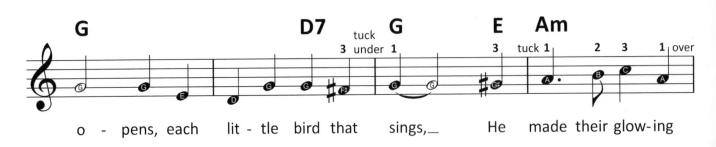

o - pens, each lit - tle bird that sings,___ He made their glow-ing

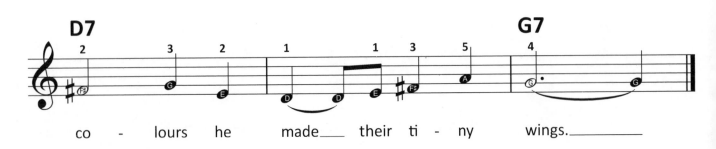

co - lours he made___ their ti - ny wings._____

Song Of The Volga Boatmen

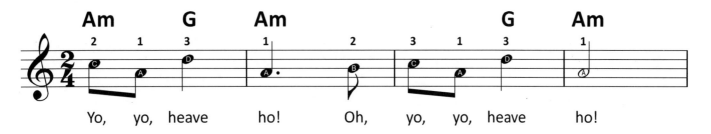

Yo, yo, heave ho! Oh, yo, yo, heave ho!

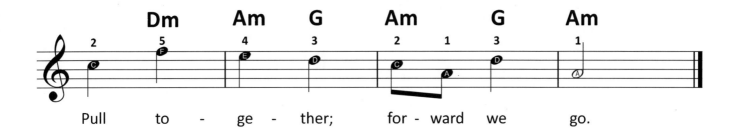

Pull to - ge - ther; for - ward we go.

Dear Liza

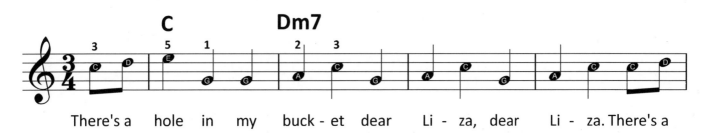

There's a hole in my buck - et dear Li - za, dear Li - za. There's a

hole in my buck - et dear Li - za a hole.

Amazing Grace

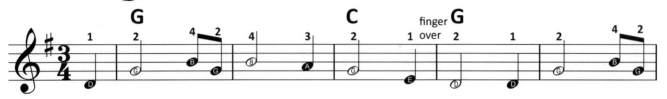

A - maz - ing__ grace, how sweet the sound that saved a____

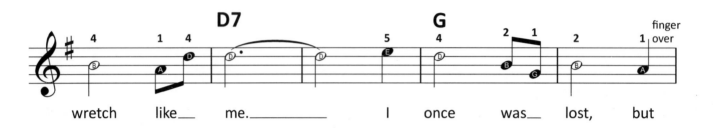

wretch like__ me._____ I once was__ lost, but

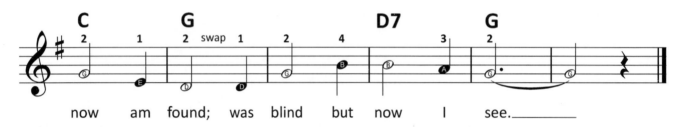

now am found; was blind but now I see._____

My Bonnie

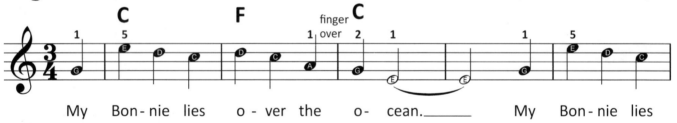

My Bon - nie lies o - ver the o - cean._____ My Bon - nie lies

o - ver the sea._____ My Bon - nie lies o - ver the o - cean,__

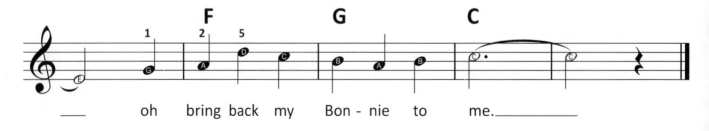

___ oh bring back my Bon - nie to me._____

I Saw Three Ships

I saw three ships come sail - ing in, on Christ - mas

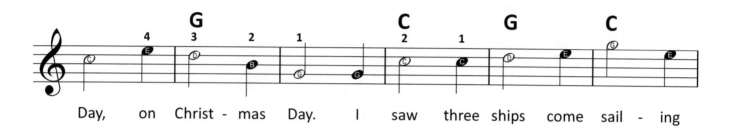

Day, on Christ - mas Day. I saw three ships come sail - ing

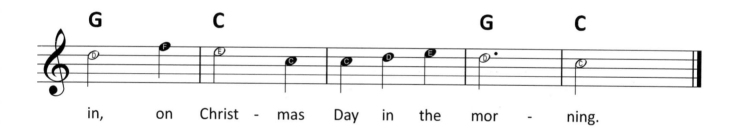

in, on Christ - mas Day in the mor - ning.

Au Clare De La Lune

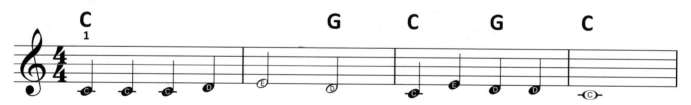

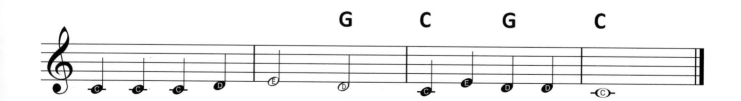

Swing Low, Sweet Chariot

Swing low sweet cha - ri - ot,____

com - ing for to car - ry me home. Swing__ low sweet

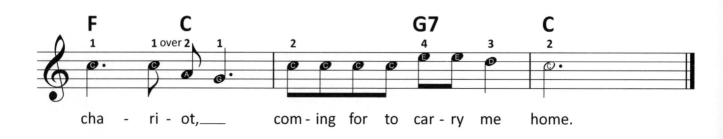

cha - ri - ot,___ com - ing for to car - ry me home.

Kumbaya

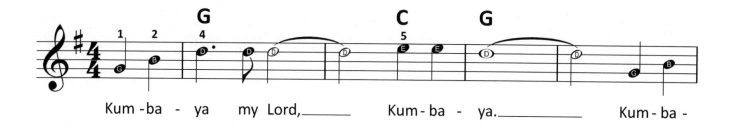

Kum - ba - ya my Lord,_____ Kum - ba - ya._____ Kum - ba -

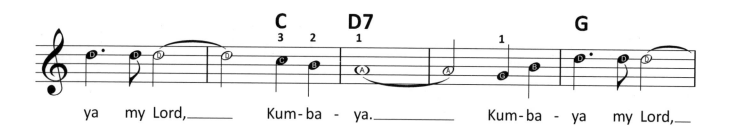

ya my Lord,_____ Kum - ba - ya._____ Kum - ba - ya my Lord,__

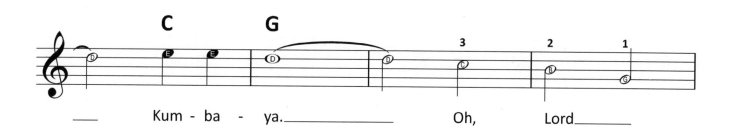

__ Kum - ba - ya._____ Oh, Lord_____

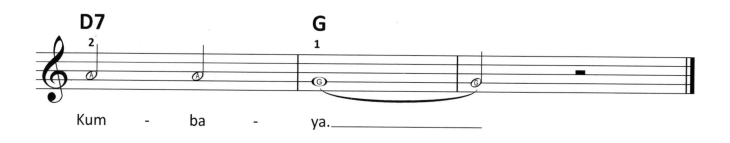

Kum - ba - ya._____

Streets Of Laredo

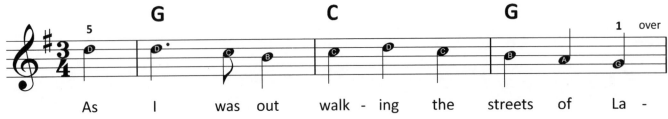

As I was out walk - ing the streets of La -

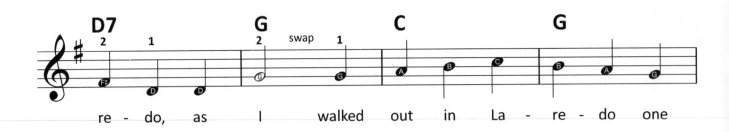

re - do, as I walked out in La - re - do one

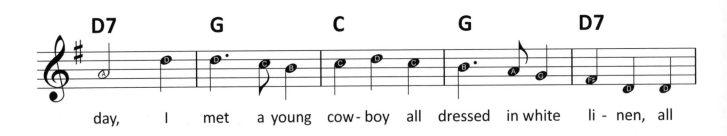

day, I met a young cow - boy all dressed in white li - nen, all

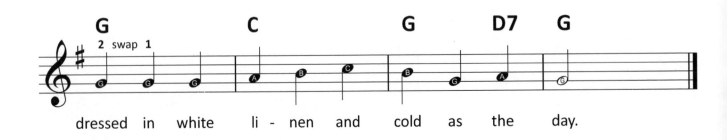

dressed in white li - nen and cold as the day.

Silent Night

Oh, Susanna

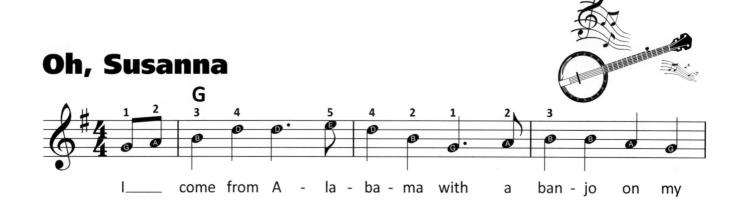

I___ come from A - la - ba - ma with a ban - jo on my

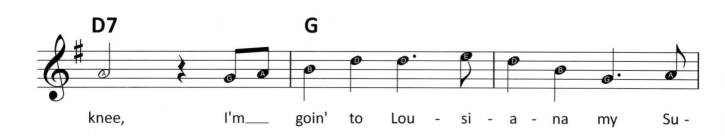

knee, I'm___ goin' to Lou - si - a - na my Su -

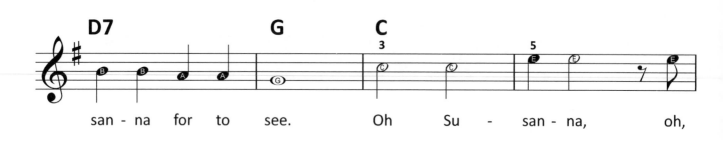

san - na for to see. Oh Su - san - na, oh,

don't you cry for me, for I come from A - la -

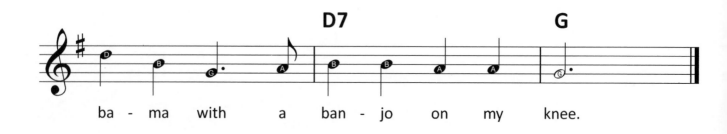

ba - ma with a ban - jo on my knee.

Ode To Joy

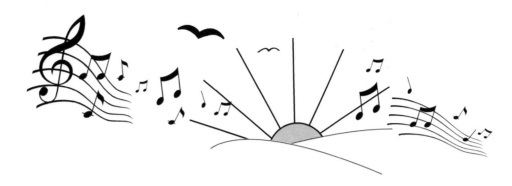

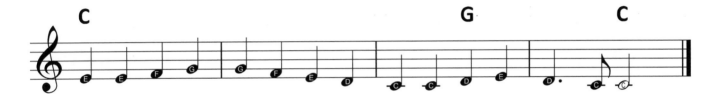

Drink To Me Only

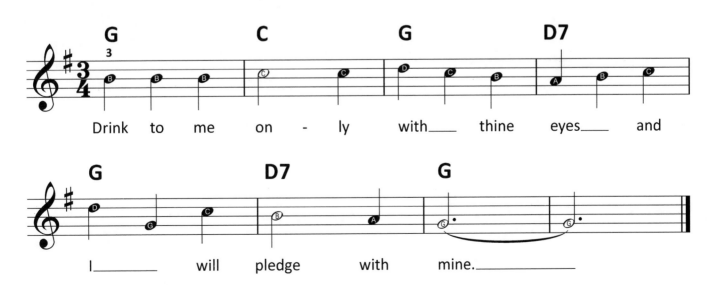

Drink to me on - ly with___ thine eyes___ and

I___ will pledge with mine.___

We Wish You A Merry Christmas

We wish you a mer - ry Christ - mas, we

wish you a mer - ry Christ - mas, we wish you a mer - ry

Christ - mas and a hap - py new year. We/Glad

ti - dings we bring to you and the king. We

wish you a mer - ry Christ - mas and a hap - py new year.

Oh Little Town Of Bethlehem

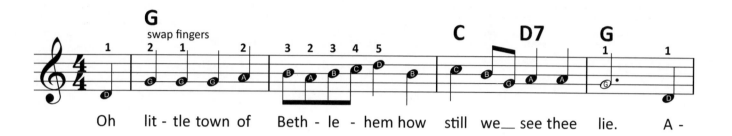

Oh lit - tle town of Beth - le - hem how still we__ see thee lie. A -

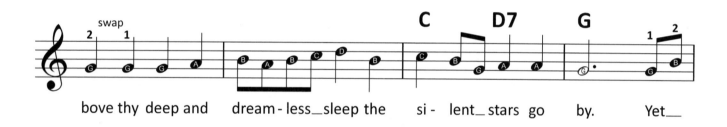

bove thy deep and dream - less__ sleep the si - lent__ stars go by. Yet__

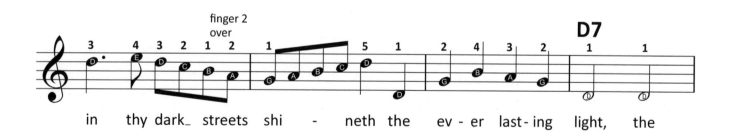

in thy dark__ streets shi - neth the ev - er last - ing light, the

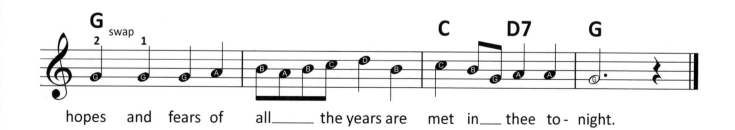

hopes and fears of all_____ the years are met in__ thee to - night.

Good King Wenceslas

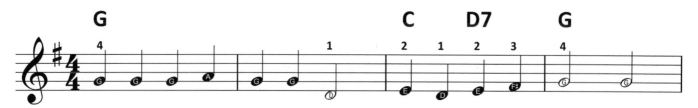

Good King Wen - ces - las looked out   on the feast of   Ste - phen,

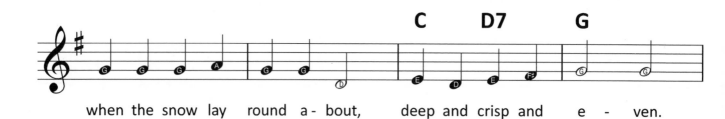

when the snow lay round a- bout,   deep and crisp and   e - ven.

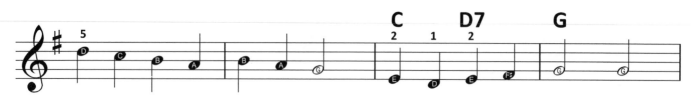

Bright - ly shone the   moon that night,   though the frost was   cru - el.

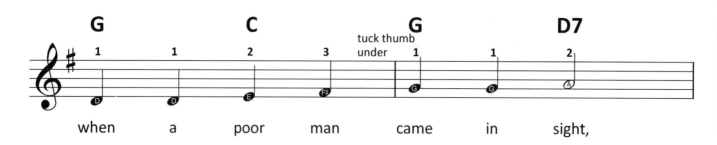

when   a   poor   man   came   in   sight,

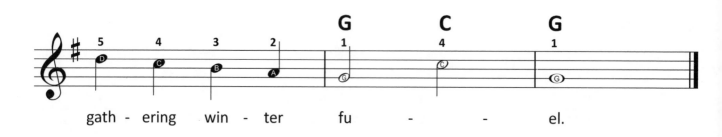

gath - ering   win - ter   fu - - el.

We Three Kings Of Orient Are

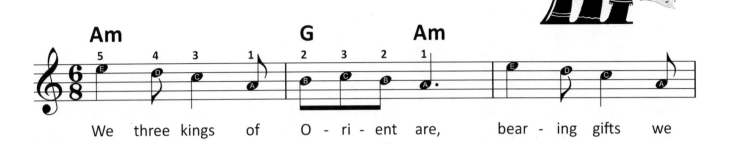

We three kings of O - ri - ent are, bear - ing gifts we

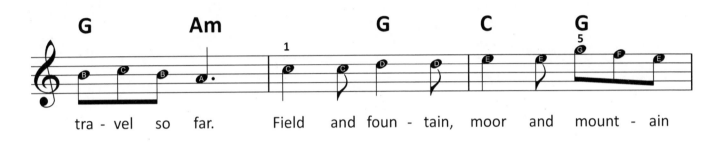

tra - vel so far. Field and foun - tain, moor and mount - ain

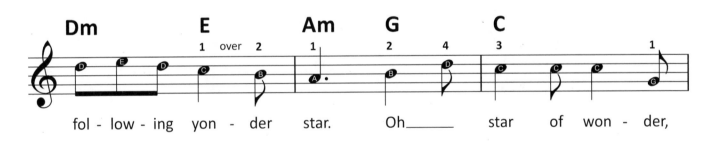

fol - low - ing yon - der star. Oh_____ star of won - der,

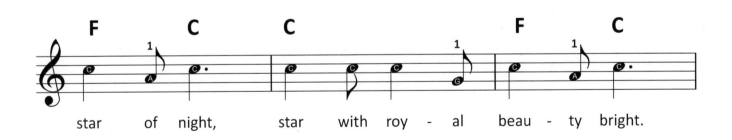

star of night, star with roy - al beau - ty bright.

West - ward lead - ing, still pro - ceed - ing, guide us to thy per - fect light.

MORE GREAT MUSIC BOOKS FROM KYLE CRAIG!

How To Play UKULELE — A Complete Guide for Absolute Beginners

978-1-908-707-08-6

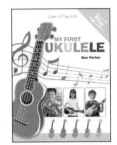

My First UKULELE — Learn to Play: Kids

978-1-908-707-11-6

Easy UKULELE Tunes

978-1-908707-37-6

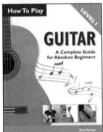

How To Play GUITAR — A Complete Guide for Absolute Beginners

978-1-908-707-09-3

My First GUITAR — Learn to Play: Kids

978-1-908-707-13-0

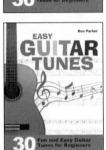

Easy GUITAR Tunes

978-1-908707-34-5

How To Play KEYBOARD — A Complete Guide for Absolute Beginners

978-1-908-707-14-7

My First KEYBOARD — Learn to Play: Kids

978-1-908-707-15-4

Easy KEYBOARD Tunes

978-1-908707-35-2

How To Play PIANO — A Complete Guide for Absolute Beginners

978-1-908-707-16-1

My First PIANO — Learn to Play: Kids

978-1-908-707-17-8

Easy PIANO Tunes

978-1-908707-33-8

How To Play HARMONICA — A Complete Guide for Absolute Beginners

978-1-908-707-28-4

My First RECORDER — Learn to Play: Kids

978-1-908-707-18-5

Easy RECORDER Tunes

978-1-908707-36-9

How To Play BANJO — A Complete Guide for Absolute Beginners

978-1-908-707-19-2

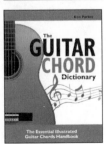

The GUITAR Chord Dictionary

978-1-908707-39-0

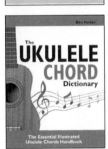

The UKULELE Chord Dictionary

978-1-908707-38-3